Ripley's Believe It or Not!

Developed and produced by Ripley Publishing Ltd

This edition published and distributed by:

Mason Crest
370 Reed Road, Broomall, Pennsylvania 19008
www.masoncrest.com

Printed and bound in the United States of America.

First printing
9 8 7 6 5 4 3 2 1

Ripley's Believe It or Not!
World Wonders
ISBN-13: 978-1-4222-2576-9 (hardcover)
ISBN-13: 978-1-4222-9251-8 (e-book)
Ripley's Believe It or Not!—Complete 16 Title Series
ISBN-13: 978-1-4222-2560-8

Library of Congress Cataloging-in-Publication Data

World wonders.
    p. cm. – (Ripley's believe it or not!)
ISBN 978-1-4222-2576-9 (hardcover) – ISBN 978-1-4222-2560-8 (series hardcover) –
ISBN 978-1-4222-9251-8 (ebook)
1. Curiosities and wonders–Juvenile literature. I. Title: World wonders.
AG243.P674 2012
031.02–dc23
                    2012020385

PUBLISHER'S NOTE
While every effort has been made to verify the accuracy of the entries in this book, the Publisher's cannot be held responsible for any errors contained in the work. They would be glad to receive any information from readers.

WARNING
Some of the stunts and activities in this book are undertaken by experts and should not be attempted by anyone without adequate training and supervision.

Ripley's Believe It or Not!

Disbelief and Shock!

WORLD WONDERS

www.MasonCrest.com

WORLD WONDERS

Extreme Earth. Open up a global mix of natural oddities, fantastic festivals, and incredible buildings. Read about the Mexican cave that is home to giant 35-ft-long (11-m) crystals, the annual Monkey Buffet Festival in Thailand, and the house that is shaped like a toilet seat.

This art installation in Liverpool, England, can turn itself inside out.

Birth of an Island

While sailing in the Vava'u group of islands Fredrik Fransson amazingly came across an island being formed right in front of his eyes!

Fredrik with the yacht Maiken anchored behind him.

FREDRIK FRANSSON ONBOARD YACHT MAIKEN
BRISBANE, AUSTRALIA
AUGUST 11, 2006

We left Neiafu in the Vava'u group of islands in the northern part of Tonga on Friday, August 11, sailing toward Fiji. There was no wind, so we motored along toward an offshore island called Late Island.

Fairly soon we discovered brown grainy streaks in the water. It looked like heavy oil mixed with water. The surrounding water was strangely greenish, like a lagoon, not the deep bluish color that you normally see sailing offshore. As we got further southwest, the streaks turned into heavy bands of floating matter, until the whole horizon was a solid line that looked like a desert.

So far we didn't have a problem, as it was such a thin layer on the surface that it got pushed away by the bow wave, but when we entered the solid field it started to pile up and behaved like wet concrete. The sight was unbelievable; it looked like rolling sand dunes as far as the eye could see. Our speed went from 7 knots down to 1 knot as the pumice stones dragged along the waterline.

A field of pumice appears to rise out of the deep blue sea.

We turned around as quickly as we could and headed back the same way we came, toward clear water. As we hit clear water, we turned off the engine and figured out that it must have come from a volcanic eruption somewhere near. We were too far from land to contact anyone on the VHF radio, so our only options were either to sail south along the pumice rafts or to head back to the islands. I wanted to make sure that everything was OK with the boat before heading off for a longer passage, so we decided to head back toward land and anchor for the night.

The wake of the sailboat made a dramatic course through the volcanic pumice stones as Fransson steered through them.

curiosity overcame us and we headed toward the southern part of Home reef. The closer we came to the island, the clearer the smoke stood out from the surrounding clouds, and every so often a massive black pillar shot upward toward the sky. You could see particles raining down.

As the wind was pushing the volcanic smoke to the northwest, we decided to go in a bit closer. While the sun was going down, we motored up to within 1½ nautical miles of the island. Later, I put the coordinates to be 18°59.55 and 174°46.3W. The island was smoldering with steam, but it was possible to get a good picture of it.

You could clearly see the three mounds creating a crater with one side breaking off and opening up toward the sea. It looked like a big island made of black coal. We reached down and felt the water and it was warmer. Our concern at the time was to sail away from the island before it got too dark, as we didn't know if we would run into more pumice rafts.

AUGUST 12, 2006

We motored out early the next morning heading south-southwest until we encountered the pumice rafts and sailed along them until they were so broken up that we could safely steer through them. We collected a few stones, some as big as a soccer ball, but the bigger they were the more brittle they were, and with the motion of the sailboat they eventually broke into pieces.

Soon we could make out that one of the clouds on the horizon wasn't a cloud but actually a smoke stack from the active volcano. The two areas of volcanic activity in the area are Metis shoal and Home reef and the smoke came from the Home reef area. We were planning to sail south of both these areas, but

The volcanic eruption sent pillars of smoke and particles into the air, but the new island was easily visible across the water.

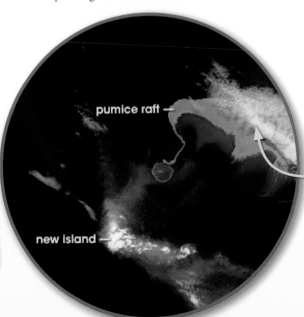

pumice raft —

new island —

When we were leaving Fiji in the middle of September, we heard on the radio an account of the pumice drifting up on beaches in Fiji. I have been told by another scientist at NASA that sometimes these islands do "disappear" with time as wind and wave action break them down. But the island that we found still shows up clearly on a satellite photo taken in the middle of October, so who knows.

This image from NASA taken in August shows the new island partially hidden by the plume of smoke erupting from the volcano. The pumice can clearly be seen.

MONSTER MUSHROOM

A monster white mushroom standing 27 in (70 cm) tall and weighing 41 lb (20 kg) was discovered growing near a coffee farm in Chiapas, southern Mexico, in 2007. The prize specimen of *Macrocybe titans* had grown to twice its normal size.

LOTTERY TREE

People in Thailand flocked to visit a banana tree in Koh Sireh in 2007 in the belief that it could predict winning lottery numbers. Many claimed to have won prizes after rubbing a mixture of powder and water on the tree's trunk, then waiting to see what number the dried solution resembled.

IRON-EATING TREE

A sycamore tree in Scotland has literally "swallowed up" pieces of metal over the past 200 years. The Brig o'Turk iron-eating tree has engulfed all kinds of scrap left by the local blacksmith and has even enveloped a bicycle that a boy left against the tree when he failed to return from World War I.

SUDDEN DEATH

The rare *Puya raimondii* plant of Bolivia can take up to 150 years to bloom—and as soon as it does, it dies.

SPORE RELEASE

If a raindrop or a passing animal hits the giant puffball fungus, thousands of spores are puffed out of a hole in the top. In a single day, a giant puffball can release as many as seven billion spores.

CORK SOURCE

Every nine years since 1820, the Whistler tree of Portugal has had its bark harvested for making corks—yielding enough to cork up to 100,000 wine bottles in a single harvest.

FIRST RAIN

After two years of abundant rain, grass began to grow for the first time ever on the desert-themed golf course at Cameron's Corner, Australia, in 2007. The unique course straddles three states—South Australia, Queensland, and New South Wales.

Ripley's research

The "hair" on the stone is thought to be the remains of a type of fungus that has been attached to its surface for hundreds of millions of years. Over that period, it has gradually extended upright and evolved into a hollow, pipe-shaped invertebrate fossil that resembles strands of white hair.

HAIRY STONE

A stone with thousands of 6-in-long (15-cm) strands of white hair growing on its surface went on display in Dalian, China, in 2005. The stone, which measured 8 in (20 cm) long and 6 in (15 cm) in diameter, was considered to be so rare that it was valued at $1,300,000.

THUNDERSTRUCK
Approximately 1,800 thunderstorms take place across the Earth at any given moment, and the planet is struck by an average of more than 100 lightning bolts every second.

STORM POWER
A single lightning strike has enough energy to light 150 million lightbulbs. An average storm can discharge sufficient power to supply the entire United States with electricity for 20 minutes.

HUGE HARVEST
A tomato tree at Walt Disney World's Epcot Center in Orlando, Florida, boasts a one-year harvest of more than 32,000 tomatoes with a total weight of 1,152 lb (522 kg).

NOISY GROWTH
The Lady in the Veil mushroom from tropical Africa takes just 20 minutes to attain its full height of 8 in (20 cm). To achieve this, its cells expand at such a rate that they make an audible cracking sound.

RARE SNOWFALL
When snow fell in Buenos Aires in July 2007, it was the Argentine capital's first major snowfall since 1918. Thousands of people cheered and threw snowballs in the streets.

TRIFFID FIND
A dandelion discovered in Hampstead, New Hampshire, in 2007, stood a monstrous 49 in (1.2 m) tall—at least five times the height of the average dandelion plant.

ARABIAN CYCLONE
The first documented cyclone ever to hit the Arabian Sea landed in Oman on June 6, 2007, with maximum sustained winds of 92.5 mph (148 km/h) and affected more than 20,000 people.

EXPLODING FRUIT
When the fruit of the South American sandbox tree is ripe, it explodes with such force that the seeds can scatter nearly 200 ft (60 m) from the main trunk. The noise of the explosion fools some people into mistaking it for gunfire.

TAP TREE
In April 2006, a tree in San Antonio, Texas, began to spout a constant flow of clean, drinkable water. People visited the tree in the hope that it held miraculous healing powers and was spouting holy water, but it turned out that it had somehow tapped its roots into an underground water pipe.

TREE-MENDOUS SHOCK
When a 200-year-old chestnut tree was felled near the town of Bournemouth in Dorset, England, in 2007, villagers were amazed to find a perfect image of a tiny tree imprinted throughout the branch and trunk. Experts said the unusual phenomenon was caused by wood rot.

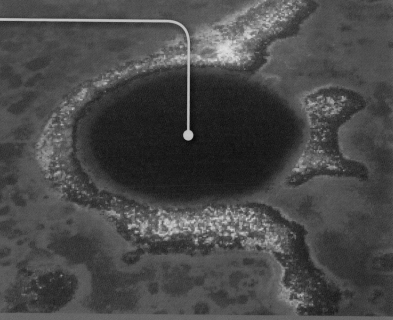

BLUE HOLE

Located on the undersea Lighthouse Reef some 60 mi (100 km) from Belize in Central America is a perfectly circular Blue Hole that measures 1,000 ft (305 m) across and 400 ft (123 m) deep. Filled with dark blue water, the hole was formed 15,000 years ago during the Ice Age when sea levels were lowered by more than 350 ft (107 m), exposing the limestone rock. As freshwater began flowing through the limestone deposits, huge underground caverns formed. Then, as the ocean began to rise again, the caverns flooded and the roof of one cavern collapsed to create this incredible sinkhole. With its breathtaking collection of stalactites, the Blue Hole is now a popular diving venue. At a depth of 130 ft (40 m) the temperature inside the hole is a constant 76°F (24°C).

FOG FOREST
A lush forest survives in Oman's Dhofar mountains with no rain! The cloud forest is surrounded by deserts and gets most of its water from seasonal fog.

WORM SHOWER
Clumps of live worms fell from the sky onto the streets of Jennings, Louisiana, in July 2007. They are thought to have been sucked up into the air by a waterspout seen 5 mi (8 km) away, and then dropped on the town.

TROPICAL ALASKA
It once topped 100°F in Alaska! On June 27, 1915, a temperature of 100°F (38°C) was recorded at Fort Yukon.

DRIFTING APART
North America and Europe are moving away from each other at about the same speed as a human fingernail grows—about 6 ft (1.8 m) every 75 years.

PURE GOLD
A lump of pure gold that is only as big as a matchbox can be flattened into a sheet the size of a tennis court. An ounce (28 g) of gold can be stretched into a wire 50 mi (80 km) long.

UNLUCKY STRIKE
A diver was killed in the ocean off Deerfield Beach, Florida, in 2007 after lightning struck his oxygen tank as he came to the surface.

UNDERWATER MOUNTAINS
The longest mountain range in the world is underwater. The Mid-Ocean Ridge extends about 40,000 mi (65,000 km) from the Arctic Ocean via the Atlantic to the Pacific off the west coast of North America.

SAFETY SALT
Ten per cent of all the salt mined in the world each year is used to de-ice freezing roads in North America.

ALASKAN TSUNAMI
In 1958, an earthquake followed by a rockslide in Lituya Bay, Alaska, triggered a huge tsunami more than 1,720 ft (525 m) high. As the area is relatively isolated and enclosed, the only casualties were two men in a fishing boat.

BOAT REVEALED
In April 2007, an earthquake near the Solomon Islands, measuring a powerful 8.1 on the Richter scale, pushed coral reefs around 10 ft (3 m) above sea level. It also tossed up a World War II torpedo boat that had previously sunk.

HOT BLAST
In July 1949, a sudden blast of hot air swept across an area of Portugal, causing temperatures to soar remarkably from 100 to 150°F (38 to 65°C) in just two minutes. The heat surge killed countless chickens on local farms.

CRYSTAL CAVE

Mexico's Cueva de los Cristales (Crystal Cave) is home to giant gypsum crystals that are more than 35 ft (11 m) long—over one third as long as the cave itself. By studying fluid samples embedded inside the crystals in the 970-ft-deep (290-m) cave, scientists believe the mammoth structures developed because the temperature there remained just below 136°F (58°C) for hundreds of thousands of years. Volcanic activity created the Naica Mountain some 26 million years ago and filled it with high-temperature anhydrite, which is gypsum without water. Above 136°F anhydrite is stable, but below that it turns to gypsum and, in this case, has formed majestic crystals.

SNOW
DONUTS

High in Washington Pass, Washington State, in March 2007, avalanche-control expert Mike Stanford found a series of perfectly shaped frozen snow donuts. They had rolled down the mountainside and frozen in place, the biggest being about 24 in (60 cm) high, large enough for Stanford to put his head through the hole in the middle.

Ripley's research

Snow donuts—or snow rollers—are rare phenomena that form at the base of steep slopes. When a clump of soft snow falls from a tree or off a rock face into hard-packed snow, and if conditions and temperature are just right, as gravity takes over, it pulls the snow down the slope and it rolls back on itself. Usually the center collapses and creates what is called a pinwheel, but if the hole stays open, it forms a snow donut.

RAINBOW ROCK

In a stunning natural spectacle, the earth at Chamarel, Mauritius, is divided into seven colors—red, brown, violet, yellow, deep purple, blue, and green. The phenomenon, which is at its most vivid at sunrise, is the result of mineral-rich volcanic rock cooling at uneven temperatures. Bizarrely, the different colors never merge even when it rains, and if mixed together artificially in a test tube, they separate into seven distinct colors again a few days later.

FOG PARTICLES
Particles of fog are so tiny that it would take seven billion of them to fill a teaspoon.

CHICKENS PLUCKED
A tornado in Britain traveled a distance of 100 mi (160 km) on May 21, 1950. The four-hour-long storm actually plucked some chickens completely bare.

ROOFS RIPPED
Lead nails ripped from roofs by a tornado were hammered by the wind into beams many yards away at Runanga, New Zealand, on April 20, 1956.

FOREST FLATTENED
A meteor exploded over Siberia's Tunguska River on June 30, 1908, unleashing the energy of 1,000 Hiroshima bombs and flattening 770 sq mi (2,000 sq km) of forest.

TOWN RESURFACES
Nearly 50 years after being submerged by the creation of an artificial lake, the underwater town of Adaminaby in Australia resurfaced following a prolonged drought in the area. The town was relocated in 1958 when Lake Eucumbene was created as part of the Snowy Mountains Hydro-Electric Scheme. Around 100 buildings were moved to the site of the new town on higher ground, some 300 mi (480 km) southwest of Sydney, but in February 2007 the lake's water level fell so much that the ruins of the old town became visible again.

WIDELY DISTRIBUTED
Gold has been located on 90 percent of the Earth's surface and is, with the exception of iron, the most broadly distributed metal on the planet. Gold is mined in such diverse settings as deserts, mountain ranges, the tropics, and the Arctic.

COLORED SNOW
Yellow snow and then red snow fell on areas of Russia within a few weeks of each other in 2006. The yellow blizzard was caused by airborne pollution from a gas and oil factory, and the red snow was the result of sandstorms in the neighboring country of Mongolia.

ICE BLOCK
In January 2007, a massive block of ice—thought to be a hailstone weighing more than 50 lb (22 kg)—fell from the sky and crushed a car belonging to Andre Javange in Tampa, Florida.

THICK ICE
Ninety percent of the world's total amount of ice is in Antarctica and at the South Pole where it is nearly 2 mi (3.2 km) thick.

OCEAN PRESSURE
The water pressure at the ocean floor, 2½ mi (4 km) deep, is equivalent to sitting under 14 fully loaded cement trucks.

COLORED POOLS

Scattered along the salt flats on the coast of Senegal are a series of small pools filled with different colored water, including red, orange, black, and white. They have been created by women workers digging for salt, which they collect by hand, load into sacks, and sell to neighboring countries. The variety of colors is a result of the high mineral concentration in the soil, the colors being intensified by the shallowness of the water in the pools.

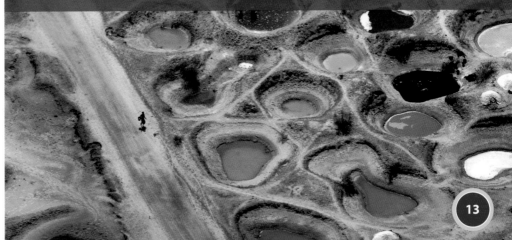

When the ovoid is closed, you would never guess that part of this building turns itself inside out.

Inside Out

An art installation in Liverpool, England, allows visitors to see a section of a building turning itself inside out. Called "Turning the Place Over" and designed by Richard Wilson, it consists of an ovoid 26 ft (8 m) in diameter, which has been cut from the façade of a derelict building in the city center and placed on a pivot. Dramatically, the ovoid rotates three-dimensionally like a huge opening and closing window.

The unusual installation seen part way through its rotation.

WEALTHY TIMES
Businesses on Times Square in New York City generate about $55 billion a year in revenue—enough to make the city block the world's 76th largest economy.

PAINTED MOUNTAIN
In 2007, forestry officials in Yunnan, China, hired seven workers to spray-paint parts of Laoshou Mountain green. The barren patch of land had been left an eyesore by years of quarrying, but instead of planting trees, the county government decided to paint the mountainside.

NAME GAME
Citizens in Wisconsin couldn't agree on a name for their small town, so they decided to pull six letters out of a hat and name it whatever those letters spelled. Thus the town of Ixonia was born!

GOOD VIBRATIONS
The Brentwood Baptist Deaf Church in Brentwood, Tennessee, uses speakers under the floor to allow its congregants to "hear" the music through the vibrations that transmit through their feet into their bodies.

MECHANICAL MAN
In Calgary, Alberta, Canada, there is a 27-ft (8.2-m) mechanical man called Spike, made from locomotive and freight car parts. His body is a boiler, his head and ears are gears, his arms and hands are couplers, and he holds a crankshaft in his right hand.

BIG CHEESE
A concrete cheese—6 ft (1.8 m) high and 28 ft (8.5 m) in circumference—sits at Perth, Ontario, Canada, to commemorate the mammoth cheese produced in the town for the 1893 Chicago World's Fair. The real cheese weighed 22,000 lb (9,780 kg) and was made using one day's milk from 10,000 cows. It created such a stir that, in 1943, it was decided to build an exact concrete replica.

PLANE COMFORT
The Woodlyn Park Motel at Waitamo, New Zealand, offers accommodation in an old freight airplane that supplied U.S. troops in Vietnam, a railway carriage, or a range of hobbit houses! The Bristol Freighter plane has been converted into two rooms, and guests are able to sleep in a bed directly under the cockpit.

EXTRA BOUNCE
Pedestrians across the United States are feeling an extra spring in their step thanks to rubber sidewalks. Rubber panels have been tested in a number of cities—including Santa Monica, California, and Seattle, Washington—to determine whether or not they are a viable alternative to concrete.

BIG FOOT
The Golden Driller statue, dedicated to the oil industry in Tulsa, Oklahoma, stands 76 ft (23 m) tall and has size 393 DD shoes!

MONSTER GRASSHOPPER
The town of Wilkie, Saskatchewan, Canada, is home to an unusual monument—a wooden grasshopper measuring 18 x 6 ft (5.5 x 1.8 m) and weighing 4,000 lb (1,815 kg).

WINE BARRELS
A number of old wine-making barrels have been converted into bedrooms at a hotel in Stavoren, the Netherlands. The 3,830-gal (14,500-l) wooden barrels are large enough to accommodate two single beds, a small living room with TV, and a bathroom with shower and toilet.

REVOLVING HOTEL

Located in Mahallesi, Turkey, is the world's only revolving hotel, giving guests in 24 bedrooms a 360-degree view. Powered by six electric motors in the basement, full rotation of the 2,750-ton building takes between two and 22 hours.

WEIGHTY PROBLEM

The Vatican Library in Rome, Italy, closed for the first time in its 530-year history in 2007 while workers repaired the damage caused by the weight of nearly two million manuscripts.

DANCING HOUSE

Designed by Czech architect Vlado Miluni and Canadian Frank Gehry, the Dancing House in Prague is so-called because it is shaped like Fred Astaire and Ginger Rogers dancing together. The building, which was completed in 1996, acquires its unusual curves from 99 concrete panels, each a different shape and size.

SHOE HOUSE

A house near Branddraai, South Africa, is built in the shape of a giant lace-up shoe. Designed by artist Ron van Zyl in 1990, the shoe house has its entrance in the two-story heel and accommodation in the toe.

ROBOT BANK

Asked to come up with a futuristic design for the Bank of Asia building in Bangkok, Thailand, architect Sumet Jumsai took inspiration from his son's toy robot. The 20-story building is shaped like a giant robot and even has two 20-ft (6-m) lidded "eyes" that serve as windows on the top floor. The eyeballs are made of glass and the lids are metal louvers.

PORCELAIN PALACE

A newly opened house in Tianjin, China, has more than 400 million pieces of porcelain inlaid everywhere in the architecture. Businessman Zhang Lianzhi spent $65 million decorating the China House with items he has collected over the past two decades, including 16,000 items of ancient chinaware made up of bowls, dishes, figurines, and vases.

CUBAN PARK

The José Martí Park in Ybor City, Florida, is actually owned by Cuba. Named after the Cuban writer and independence leader, the park was purchased by Cuba in 1957.

LUXURY LIFEBOAT

A lifeboat moored in Harlingen, the Netherlands, has been converted into a luxury hotel. The Lilla Marras carried out 105 sea rescues between 1955 and 1979, saving 45 lives, and because it is still seaworthy, guests can pay to be taken out to sea.

VIOLIN HALL

The Chowdiah Memorial Hall in Bangalore, India, was built in 1980 in the shape of a giant violin to honor the master violinist Tirumakudalu Chowdiah.

MOLE MAN

Bruce Tracy, a construction worker, builds secret underground living quarters for himself and other homeless people in Fresno, California.

LEANING STEEPLE

A 15th-century church steeple in Suurhusen, Germany, stands 84 ft (26 m) high and leans at an angle of five degrees—a degree more than Italy's famous Leaning Tower of Pisa.

MIGHTY MUSKIE

The National Freshwater Fishing Hall of Fame Museum in Hayward, Wisconsin, is housed in a building the shape of a huge muskie fish. The monumental muskie is 143 ft (44 m) long and 41 ft (12 m) high.

The Blind Adventurer

Miles Hilton-Barber during his mammoth trek across Antarctica's frozen landscape.

In April 2007, Miles Hilton-Barber piloted a tiny micro-light aircraft on a 13,360-mi (21,500-km) flight from London, England, to Sydney, Australia. The epic journey took him 55 days and involved 118 stops—but what made it truly remarkable is that Miles is blind.

The 59-year-old from Derbyshire, England, is no stranger to great adventures. Over the past decade he has circumnavigated the globe, climbed some of the world's highest mountains, trekked 150 mi (240 km) across the Sahara Desert, hauled a sled 250 mi (400 km) across Antarctica, and completed more than 40 parachute jumps.

Miles was inspired by his blind brother Geoff, who sailed solo from South Africa to Australia in 1999. "That's what made me realize the problem in my life wasn't my blindness," he says, "it was my attitude to it. The only thing holding me back was five inches—the distance between my ears."

Accompanied by sighted friend Jon Cook, Miles, who has been blind for more than 25 years, has climbed to a height of 17,500 ft (5,335 m) in the Himalayas as well as scaling Mount Kilimanjaro and Mont Blanc, the highest mountains in Africa and Europe respectively.

In 2001, Miles ran the 11-day Ultra-Marathon race across China, and the following year he completed the Siberian Ice Marathon, known as "The Coldest Marathon on Earth." Within weeks he was crossing the entire Qatar Desert nonstop in 78 hours—day and night—without sleep.

Accompanied by two disabled friends, he set off on a 93-day, 38,000-mi (61,155-km) circumnavigation of the globe in 2003, using more than 80 challenging forms of transport. These included a hot-air balloon to get him over the Nevada Desert, an elephant, and a racing car driven at 125 mph (200 km/h).

Four years later, accompanied by sighted copilot Richard Meredith-Hardy, Miles made the micro-light flight from England to Australia, flying over 21 countries and combating freezing temperatures and tropical thunderstorms along the way. Reflecting on his many adventures, he says: "The only limits in our lives are those we set for ourselves."

Miles (left) and his companion Jon Cook trek across Antarctica.

Miles (left) riding an ostrich in South Africa during his circumnavigation of the globe in 2003.

The amazing micro-light flight from London to Sydney fulfilled another ambition for Miles. "Since I was a kid I wanted to be a pilot," he says. "Then I went blind and they said I'd never fly."

Miles goes on an underwater scuba walk in the Red Sea, accompanied by his paraplegic friend Mike Mackenzie.

Climbing the icy ridges of the Cairngorms in Scotland presented a formidable challenge for Miles (right) and his sighted guide Jon Cook.

Miles rappelling down Table Mountain in Cape Town, South Africa. He was the first blind person ever to achieve this feat.

MAGNIFICENT MUMMIES

More than 2,000 human mummies line the walls of an underground crypt in Palermo, Sicily —all wearing their finest clothes. To make the spectacle even spookier, their jaws are loosely wired in place so that their mouths appear to be gaping wide at visitors.

Some are stretched out in niches carved into the limestone of the Capuchin Catacombs, but, owing to lack of space, others simply hang from hooks on the walls. The mummies are grouped according to age, sex, and social status, ranging from tiny babies in cribs and rocking chairs to adult lawyers in their best suits and soldiers in uniform. There are also hundreds of coffins, the sides of which have been cut open to reveal the deceased.

The monks of Palermo began mummifying their dead as a status symbol more than 400 years ago. The first Palermo mummification happened by chance. A monk, Brother Silvestro, died suddenly in 1599 and some months later it was found that the limestone and the lack of air in the crypt had combined to mummify his body. Thereafter, his fellow monks decided that they, too, wished to be mummified after death and soon the wealthier local townspeople began to express similar desires.

The practice was finally discontinued in the 1920s. One of the last people to be mummified was two-year-old Rosalia Lombardo, also known as the "Sleeping Beauty." Her family frequently visited her open coffin.

Although the dry air in the crypt has preserved many of the remains, body parts such as ears and hands have fallen off over the years, and other mummies are now little more than dressed skeletons.

Hundreds of dressed corpses line the walls of the crypt, having been embalmed by the Capuchin monks of the city. Surprisingly, there is no smell.

Ripley's research . . . . .

The most common form of mummification in Palermo was for the bodies to be dehydrated in special cells for eight months after death, then taken out and washed in vinegar. However, during times of epidemic, the bodies were often dipped in arsenic or lime. Dr. Salofia, the Palermo medic who tended to young Rosalia Lombardo, injected chemicals to mummify her but took the details with him to his grave.

Many local people wrote wills naming the clothes in which they wanted to be buried, or stipulated that their clothes should be changed over a period of time. The Palermo mummies are all dressed as they had been in life. Consequently, some of the mummified monks have ropes dangling from their necks, because when they were alive they had worn the ropes as a penance.

MUMMY MEDICINE
In the 16th century, mummies were thought to possess medicinal properties that could prevent wounds from bleeding. Coated in honey, they were sold in powdered form as pharmaceuticals to be taken orally.

CORPSE EXPORT
During the American Civil War, mummies were imported to the United States so that the extensive linen in which they were wrapped could be manufactured into paper.

WELL PRESERVED
The mummy of a small girl born in the 2nd century AD was so well preserved when found near Rome, Italy, some 1,800 years later, that her fingerprints could be taken.

THICK WRAPPING
An ancient Egyptian mummy had more than 9,000 sq ft (835 sq m) of wrappings.

Although the clothes of the Palermo mummies have survived the centuries, many of the bodies themselves have been reduced to skeletons.

On the better-preserved bodies in Palermo, the flesh, the hair, and even the eyes have been mummified.

The mummified body of a child in the Capuchin Catacombs at Palermo. Whereas many of the adults were simply hung in rows, some of the children were arranged to adopt specific poses.

WEIRD ENTERTAINMENT

Aristocrats in 19th-century Europe used to buy a mummy, unwrap it, and invite friends over to view the curiosity. The regular exposure to air eventually caused the mummies to disintegrate.

BURIAL JARS

A tribe from Borneo keep their dead in huge earthenware jars. As the corpse rots, the bodily fluid is drained away and the dried remains are put in another container. The original jars are then re-used for cooking.

INUIT FAMILY

Eight well-preserved, 500-year-old mummies were discovered at an Inuit settlement in Greenland in 1972—a baby, a young boy, and six women. The bodies had been mummified naturally by the sub-zero temperatures and the dry winds in the cave in which they were found.

Mummies of Capuchin monks were dressed in priestly vestments so that their colleagues could pray to them after death.

REMOTE HOTEL
Birdsville Hotel and Pub, located in Australia's Simpson Desert, is 900 mi (1,450 km) from the nearest town or city, but still serves 45,000 customers a year.

MOUNTAIN TOILETS
Two toilets have been built near the snow-covered summit of France's Mont Blanc. At 13,976 ft (4,260 m), they are the highest washrooms in Europe.

CROOKED HOUSE
A crazily shaped building in Sopot, Poland, was inspired by fairytale illustrations and has roof tiles resembling the scales of a dragon. Built in 2003, the 4,780-sq-yd (4,000-sq-m) Centrum Rezydent was created by architect Szotynscy Zaleski, who based his theme on the children's book drawings of Polish illustrator Jan Marcin Szancer. At the heart of the crooked house is a bar named Wonky Pub.

PIPE HOME
A man in China has built a home using two cement pipes—and it has become a city attraction. Xin Yucai, 50, of Shenyang City, bought two cement pipes from a construction company and turned them into a real house with windows, a door, and even a chimney. He turned down the offer of living in his daughter's apartment because he loves his new home so much.

PRISON GUESTS
A hotel in Liepaja, Latvia, offers guests the opportunity to experience life in a former Soviet prison. The old Karosta jail has been converted into a hotel, but visitors must still sleep on a barren bunk in a damp cell, scrub out the toilets, and are ordered around by the "prison" staff.

QUIET TOWN
The town of Colma, California, has fewer than 2,000 residents—but more than 1.5 million bodies in its cemeteries. Perhaps unsurprisingly, the town's motto is: "It's great to be alive in Colma!"

PRIVATE PUB
In response to a 2007 ban on smoking in public places, including bars and pubs, Kerry Morgan of Briton Ferry, Wales, built a private 90-seat pub in his home.

PINK CITY
Officials in Aurangabad in Bihar, India, painted many of the buildings in their city bright pink—thinking that it would help lower the crime rate.

MEAN MOSQUITO
In Upsala, Ontario, Canada, stands a steel and fiberglass monument of a giant mosquito carrying a man and a knife and fork! The hungry mosquito, which is 16 ft (5 m) long and has a wingspan of 15 ft (4.5 m), is holding the 6-ft (1.8-m) man with its legs.

HOUSE GIFT
Hollywood photographer Jasin Boland came up with the perfect Valentine's present for fiancée Maria Moral Pena—a gift-wrapped $1-million house. He arranged for the house—in Gloucestershire, England—to be covered in 5,000 sq ft (465 sq m) of white fabric, sprinkled with red hearts, and finished with a giant pink bow.

FLOATING SHOP
Dave's Bait House offers food, drinks, and fishing bait—all from Dave Steiner's 33-ft (10-ft) boat, which he anchors some 6 mi (9.5 km) from shore in the Gulf of Mexico.

TOILET HOME

In 2007, architect Sim Jae-duck lifted the lid on his toilet house. Built from steel, white concrete, and glass, the 4,520-sq-ft (420-sq-m) home near Seoul, South Korea, is shaped like a toilet and even has a symbolic opening in the roof. Sim, who was actually born in a restroom, designed the $1.6-million house as part of his campaign for cleaner toilets worldwide. Naturally, it has four luxury washrooms.

PINK PALACE

No two columns, doors, or even door handles are alike in the 13,155-sq-yd (11,000-sq-m) Green Citadel in Magdeburg, Germany. The last project of Austrian artist Friedensreich Hundertwasser, who died in 2000, the pink building resembles a child's drawing and, like any Hundertwasser house, there are no straight lines. The $33.8-million development—containing 55 apartments, a hotel, shops, and office space—has roofs covered in grass and the buildings are topped with gold balls.

GLASS HOUSE

The Glass House in Boswell, British Columbia, Canada, was built from half a million empty embalming-fluid bottles. It was begun in 1952 by retired undertaker David H. Brown, who traveled western Canada collecting the bottles from friends in the funeral profession and ended up with about 250 tons of them.

SECRET APARTMENT

Eight artists built and furnished a secret apartment inside a Providence, Rhode Island, shopping mall—and stayed there for four years. They used breeze blocks to build the apartment in a disused space next to a parking lot and overcame the absence of plumbing by sneaking out to use mall toilets.

SMALL HOUSE

Artist Jay Shafer of Sebastopol, California, lives in a house that is 96 sq ft (9 sq m)—smaller than many bathrooms. He built the tiny wooden house himself and wheeled it into a position overlooking an apple orchard. The advantages of a compact residence—little housework, for one—have led to him building small houses for other people, too.

Enter the Vault

HIGH FRONT DOOR

In the 1940s, Watertown, Massachusetts, was the location of this unusual front door, which had a front step 18 ft (5.5 m) above the sidewalk.

MOVING NEXT DOOR

A tornado in Lorain, Ohio, in 1928, lifted off the top story of this house and carefully set it down beside it.

TALL STORY ▶

This log cabin built in Urania, Louisiana, in the 1930s, was an astonishing 50 ft (15 m) high.

NO PARKING!

These unconventional road signs appeared on either side of a downtown street in Randolph, Vermont, in the 1980s.

REDWOOD RESIDENCE

This home in Palm Springs, California, was built in the 1950s in the shape of the famous giant redwood tree General Sherman, which stands in Sequoia National Park in California.

MINI HOSPITAL

Built in the 1930s, this veterinary hospital in New York City was once billed as the smallest in the world—it measured just 3 x 15 ft (1 x 4.5 m). Its owner, Dr. J. Lebish, had his office upstairs.

LUCKY BREAK

A tornado carried away the end of this house in Elgin, Illinois, in 1934, but left every dish in the pantry intact!

TINY CHURCH

Built in the 1930s, the Little Cathedral of Festina, in the town of Festina, Iowa, is a tiny church that seats a mere eight worshipers.

NAME THAT TOWN

In 1930, Robert Ripley visited the Welsh town that until recently had the longest town name in the world. Seen here standing at the town's railway station, Ripley was visiting Llanfairpwllgwyngyllgogerychwyrndrobwllllantysiliogogogoch, whose name translates as "The church of St. Mary in the hollow of white hazel trees near the rapid whirlpool by St. Tysilio's of the red cave."

FLOATING HOUSE

In 1940, R.G. Letourneau of Peoria, Illinois, built a house that he then towed to its destination, across the Illinois River. The watertight steel house, complete with furnace, plumbing, and furniture, did not sit on a barge, but floated happily to its new home.

BEER MOUNTAIN

When property manager Ryan Froerer went to check out one of his rented apartments in Ogden, Utah, he found around 70,000 empty beer cans piled high all the way up to the ceiling, completely obscuring the furniture. The cans, which equate to 24 beers a day during the tenant's eight-year stay, were later recycled for $800.

STRESS BUSTERS
Customers at the Rising Sun Anger Release Bar in Nanjing, China, are invited to relieve stress by smashing glasses and beating up staff, who wear protective padding.

MAGIC MENU
At the Ninja Japanese restaurant in New York City, waiters perform magic tricks while serving customers their sushi.

WEIGH-IN
The town of High Wycombe in Buckinghamshire, England, is the only place in the world that weighs its mayor publicly. Mayors are weighed at the beginning and end of their year in office to see whether or not they have gained any weight at the taxpayers' expense.

HORSESHOE TOWER
The Scarrington Horseshoe Tower in Nottinghamshire, England, is 17 ft (5 m) high and 6 ft (1.8 m) in diameter—and is made up of more than 50,000 metal horseshoes.

FINDERS KEEPERS
Diamonds State Park in Arkansas has a diamond mine where visitors can search for—and keep—any gems they find.

COOL BAR
A new bar in Dubai is the coolest place to hang out—because everything is made of ice. The bar, tables, and chairs at Chillout are made of ice, as are the cups, glasses, and plates. There is also an ice sculpture that depicts Dubai's skyline, and an ice chandelier. A cover charge provides customers with a hooded coat, woolen gloves, and insulated shoes to keep out frostbite.

DOLLHOUSE MEMORIAL
The grave of Nadine Earles (1929–33) in Lanett, Alabama, is covered by a brick dollhouse with a life-sized doll, a tea set, and toys inside.

DEEP MINE
Two of the world's tallest buildings could be stacked on top of each other in the pit of the Kennecott Copper Mine in Utah and still not reach the surface!

TAAL TALE
In the Philippines there is an island in a lake on an island in a lake on an island! The first island is in Crater Lake on Volcano Island in Lake Taal on Luzon Island.

DOLLAR BAR

A bar in the Florida Keys is dripping in money. Every wall and ceiling of the No Name Pub is plastered with dollar bills donated by customers who, for the past 20 years, have been writing their names and messages on bills and stapling them to the wall. It is estimated that the bar is now covered in an estimated $100,000 worth of cash.

DRAINPIPE HOTEL
The Dasparkhotel near Linz, Austria, consists of three big concrete drainpipes, each of which has a double bed squashed into it. Blankets, storage space, and an electrical socket are also provided. Guests pay what they think the accommodation is worth.

OIL FIELD
The grounds of the State Capitol in Oklahoma City, Oklahoma, doubled up as a working oil field during most of the 20th century.

SENIOR PLAYTIME
In 2007, Berlin's Preussen Park opened Germany's first playground for senior citizens. The playground, which is fitted with eight steel flexibility machines, is designed to encourage elderly people to keep fit, as well as to socialize.

PLASTIC HOUSE
Tomislav Radovanovic of Kragujevac, Serbia, has spent five years building a house made out of 13,500 plastic bottles. Only the foundation of the 72-sq-yd (60-sq-m) house is concrete—even the kitchen furniture and windows are made of plastic bottles.

SALMON CARE
The Chester Creek River in Westchester, Alaska, has had its gradient reduced to make it easier for the tired salmon that have to jump upstream every year to reach their breeding grounds.

COLOR CHANGE
The water in a lake in Manitoba, Canada, has the amazing ability to change color. Little Limestone Lake, which lies some 280 mi (450 km) north of Winnipeg, is a marl lake, which means that it changes color as water temperatures rise and the mineral calcite that is dissolved in the water begins to settle. So in warm, summer weather the water can go from clear to an opaque turquoise and then to a milky blue-white.

CROC DETERRENT
Crocodiles bred in captivity in eastern India have been released into the wild in order to protect endangered animals from poachers. Creatures living in wildlife sanctuaries in Orissa and West Bengal have been threatened by poachers, but the introduction of dozens more crocodiles to the sanctuaries has successfully served as a formidable deterrent.

GRUNGE PLUNGE
Mexico City's subterranean sewers are so full that a team of men must dive into bacteria-filled waters daily to prevent them from becoming clogged.

TOURISTS' REVENGE
The Scottish town of Dunoon has a unique line of souvenirs—it sells millions of dead midges every year. The irritating little insects, which bite hundreds of tourists each year, are collected and sold at £5 ($10) for a jar of 10,000.

DEATHLY PAST
San Saba High School's Rogan Field in Texas is nicknamed "The graveyard" because it was built over a cemetery—with the bodies left in place.

SOLE STUDENT
In 2007, a school in China had just one teacher and one student. The school in Dasu, Longjing, used to have more than 400 students, but many families migrated from the mountain village, leaving Li Yongchun, who has taught in that same school for more than 25 years, to teach ever-decreasing numbers.

Monkey Buffet

Monkeys are invited to dinner in Thailand. The annual Monkey Buffet Festival at the Pra Prang Sam Yot temple in Lopburi provides food and drink for the local monkey population, which numbers more than 2,000. The monkeys feast on over 4,400 lb (2,000 kg) of fruit and vegetables that are artfully presented in the deliciously edible displays.

BODY PAIN
The Hindu festival of Thaipusam in Malaysia is celebrated with devotees piercing their bodies with a variety of objects—from pins to swordfish bills.

GRAVY WRESTLING
The first-ever World Gravy Wrestling Championships were held in Lancashire, England, in 2007. Eight teams took part, wrestling each other in a swimming pool filled with lukewarm gravy!

FURNITURE RACE
Couches, chairs, toilets, baby cribs, trash cans, and even coffins are fixed to skis or snowboards and driven at breakneck speed down a snow-covered mountain in the annual Big Mountain Furniture Race. Held every April since 1970, the event at Whitefish, Montana, marks the end of the skiing season. As well as appearance and speed, points are also awarded for accuracy, as there is a target at the end of the run and competitors are scored by how close to it they can stop without actually hitting it.

DONKEY CLIMB

Runners and donkeys team up for the most arduous pack-burro race in the world, run over a rocky 29-mi (47-km) course at Fairplay, Colorado, with a climb of 3,000 ft (915 m). Each donkey must carry a miner's pack containing a pick, a shovel, and a gold pan, plus any rocks required to achieve a total weight of at least 33 lb (15 kg). A 15-ft (4.5-m) rope connects each runner and donkey.

HAMMER BLOW

Participants in Portugal's So Joo Festival express their attraction to members of the opposite sex by hitting them over the head with a large plastic hammer!

SKUNKFEST

North Ridgeville, Ohio, is home to an annual Skunk Festival that features pet skunk beauty and costume contests.

SCISSORS DANCE

This competitor at a national scissors dance contest in Lima, Peru, has livened up his act by dancing with two crates attached to hooks pierced through his skin. Other dancers perform with nails hammered into their tongue or metal wires driven through their cheeks in a true test of courage and agility. Contestants perform each dance to the accompaniment of a pair of scissors, made from two 10-in (25-cm) pieces of metal.

BURNING WHEELS

On Easter Sunday night throughout Germany, giant oak wheels—7 ft (2.1 m) in diameter and weighing 800 lb (363 kg)—are stuffed with straw, set alight, and rolled down hillsides into the valleys below. It is believed to be a good omen if the wheels are still burning when they reach the valley.

BUN SNATCH

At the Cheung Chau Bun Festival in Hong Kong, China, contestants climb a 33-ft (10-m) tower stacked with plastic buns and try to grab as many as possible in three minutes. Local belief says that the buns make sure there will be a smooth sailing and a good catch for fishing boats.

POKER RUN

Thousands of motorbike enthusiasts take part in the annual Key West Poker Run, held in Florida every September. The riders collect their playing cards at five stops between Miami and Key West before playing their hand at the final destination.

BURRY MAN

Every August, a resident of Queensferry, Scotland, dressed in white flannels and covered from head to toe with the Velcro-like burrs of the burdock plant, parades 7 mi (11 km) through the town. During the journey he drinks whisky through a straw. The Burry Man is believed to date back to a shipwreck victim who, having no clothes, dressed himself in burrs.

SHOVEL RACE

The World Snow Shovel Racing Championships were staged at Angelfire, New Mexico, for 30 years until they were cancelled in 2005 on safety grounds. Competitors sat on a snow shovel and sped for 1,000 ft (305 m) down a snow-covered mountain at speeds that exceeded 75 mph (120 km/h).

COWBOY CONVENTION

For more than 20 years, cowboys from all over the United States and abroad have assembled in Elko, Nevada, each January to read poems and tell stories as part of the National Cowboy Poetry Gathering.

CARCASS CONTEST

In the Central Asian sport of *buzkashi*, two teams of horsemen compete to grab a livestock carcass and carry it into their opponent's circle to score points.

RAIN PRAYERS

For the Tohetohe festival in Nagasaki, Japan, people wearing conical bamboo hats and straw raincoats visit dozens of homes where residents promptly drench them with water! The festival is held each January to pray for rain during the rice-planting season.

FIRE ANT FESTIVAL

The October Fire Ant Festival, at Marshall, Texas, is a celebration of all things related to the humble fire ant—including a parade where people dress up as the insects.

CHAINSAW CARVING

A sculptor wielding a chainsaw carves a bald eagle at the annual Woodsmen's Field Days festival in New York State. The chainsaw carvers are given 45 minutes to create a sculpture, at the end of which the artworks go to auction. The winner is the sculpture that attracts the highest bid.

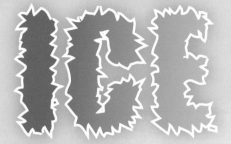

ICE WORLD

Every January, part of the northeastern Chinese city of Harbin is transformed into a beautiful ice kingdom. Teams of local and international ice sculptors create a fairytale setting of buildings, people, animals, cartoon characters, and deities using compacted snow and blocks of ice.

Snow and ice sculpting in the region dates back 1,400 years, but the Harbin Snow and Ice Festival originated in 1985. For the 2007 festival, more than 2,000 ice sculptures were crafted from more than 4 million cubic ft (120,000 cubic m) of ice and more than 3 million cubic ft (90,000 cubic m) of snow.

Each year, five million people from across the world converge on the city, drawn by the spectacular ice structures and night illuminations. Most of the sculptures are fitted with colored lights, and at night they glow red, yellow, pink, and blue.

Many of the 2007 exhibits had a Canadian theme, in honor of Canadian doctor Norman Bethune, who went to China in 1938 and is credited with introducing modern medicine into the country. There was a large ice likeness of Dr. Bethune, a model of the Chateau Frontenac in Quebec City, a snow sculpture depicting Niagara Falls that was 800 ft (244 m) long and 90 ft (27 m) high, and the Crossing of the Bering Strait built from some 460,000 cubic ft (13,000 cubic m) of snow.

Previous year's sculptures have included re-creations of the Great Wall of China and Paris's Arc de Triomphe.

Visitors to the festival can also climb a wall of solid ice, dine in a restaurant constructed from ice, and enjoy a drink in an ice bar.

In this exhibit, dead fish have been incorporated into an ice-lantern sculpture.

An ice sculpture of a girl on a swing formed part of an ice-lantern exhibition on the theme of "The World's Fairy Tales."

Ripley's research

How do they do it?

The snow and ice used in the festival are quarried from the Songhua River, where the ice can be several yards thick. Chainsaws cut through the ice and reduce it to blocks. Each team—and participants come from as far away as Canada, France, South Africa, and Russia—starts with a 10-ft (3-m) cube of packed snow and begins carving. These blocks are then fused together to make the larger sculptures.

Ordinarily, there is no danger of the creations suddenly melting, because average winter temperatures in Harbin range between –28°F (–31°C) and 5°F (–15°C). In fact, people leave stored food outside on balconies to freeze. However, as temperatures rose unexpectedly in February 2007, heads started to topple from statues, and 2,000 workers were brought in to carry out repairs.

Sculptors labored for hundreds of hours to create these superb ice replicas.

Harbin's famous St. Sophia church was one of the centerpieces of the festival.

EXPLODING ANVILS

Steel anvils are blasted up to 400 ft (120 m) through the air at Laurel, Mississippi, every April during the National Anvil Shooting Contest. Each anvil must weigh at least 100 lb (45 kg) and no more than 2 lb (1 kg) of explosives can be used to blow them up. The contest has its origins in the American Civil War when Yankee troops raided the region, blowing up anvils to destroy weapon-making facilities.

SHEEP MARCH

Bringing traffic to a standstill once a year, farmers lead some 700 sheep through the center of the Spanish capital, Madrid. The November sheep march is designed to protect Spain's 78,000 mi (125,500 km) of paths that are used for the seasonal movement of livestock.

HAIRY CONTEST

Staged at Fairbanks, Alaska, in July, the Hairy Chest, Hairy Legs, and Beard Contest sets out to find the hairiest men in the United States.

CAT LAUNCH

At the annual Flying Cat Ceremony in Verviers, Belgium, a toy cat attached to a small balloon is launched from the tower of the Church of St. Remacle. The ceremony is supposedly based on fact—in 1641 an apothecary conducted an experiment in aerodynamics by launching a live cat attached to inflated pigs' bladders from the same tower. The cat is said to have landed on its feet and run off unharmed.

MOSQUITO CALLING

The Great Texas Mosquito Festival at Clute features a mosquito-calling contest, where people are judged by their interpretations of a mosquito call, and a mosquito legs contest for the men and women with the skinniest legs. The festival is presided over by Willie Man-Chew, a 25 ft (7.6 m) mosquito in cowboy hat and boots.

MISS FATTY

A Russian youth-oriented newspaper organizes an annual beauty contest with a difference. At the Miss Fatty contest in Moscow, large ladies try to impress with their skills at such disciplines as skipping.

WORM RACE

At Banner Elk, North Carolina, each October woolly worms (a variety of furry caterpillar) crawl up a piece of string for a first prize of $1,000. The race derives from the belief that we can forecast the weather depending on the worm's ability to climb the string.

MAKING A SPLASH

In the National Cannonball Championships at Toronto, Ontario, Canada, heavyweight divers leap feet-first from a 16½-ft (5-m) tower into a swimming pool with the goal of making as big a splash as possible. Burly men plummet into the pool in a variety of costumes—including Michael Jackson, a Viking, and Princess Leia from *Star Wars*. Competitors are judged on splash, flair, and the ability to tuck.

WATER BATTLE

To cleanse the community in readiness for the Buddhist New Year, each April, around 100,000 residents of Chiang Mai, Thailand, soak each other with water pistols in a giant battle as part of the Songkran Festival.

BETTY PICNIC

An annual Betty Picnic takes place at Grants Pass, Oregon, in June to celebrate people all over the world who are called Betty or who display Betty-like characteristics!

BATHTUB REGATTA

At the International Regatta of Bathtubs—held in August on the River Meuse at Dinant, Belgium—each craft must have at least one bathtub as part of its design.

MAGIC TOUCH

In the depths of the Japanese winter, a man wearing nothing but a cotton loincloth wanders through the streets of Inazawa City, while those who try to touch him are doused by "guards" with icy water. Since 767 BC, the Naked Man has been making the journey to a local shrine, supposedly absorbing all the evil and bad luck of the people who touch him. So, every January, at a festival called Hadaka Matsuri, some 10,000 men, equally scantily clad, jostle to touch the naked man as he makes his way through the city.

CARDBOARD SLEDGES

The annual Colorado Cardboard Classic features sleds made from cardboard and glue. The 2007 event attracted 75 teams and sleds in all different shapes.

FLYING PUMPKINS

At the Punkin' Chunkin' Championship staged at Nassau, Delaware, each November, enthusiasts build catapults and mini cannons to launch their pumpkins as far as possible into the sky.

TYPEWRITER TOSS

At the annual Typewriter Toss held each April in Springfield, Missouri, contestants stand on an elevated platform and hurl their old typewriters from a height of 50 ft (15 m) at a target on the tarmac below.

FIRECRACKER TRAIL

On the last day of Chinese New Year in 2007, festival organizers in Tainan, Taiwan, lit a string of firecrackers over 8 mi (13 km) long!

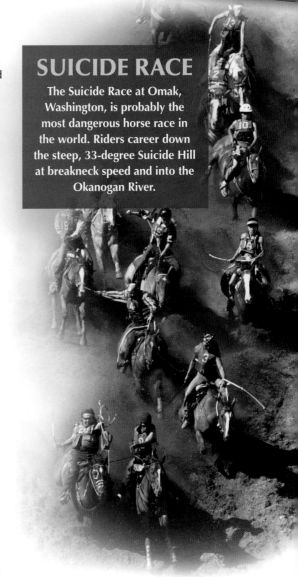

SUICIDE RACE

The Suicide Race at Omak, Washington, is probably the most dangerous horse race in the world. Riders career down the steep, 33-degree Suicide Hill at breakneck speed and into the Okanogan River.

RECKLESS ROCKETS

The Yenshui Beehive Rockets Festival in Taiwan is so dangerous that spectators wear protective clothing and crash helmets. Even so, each year, dozens of people suffer eye injuries and burns as thousands of small rockets are fired into the air and explode in a cloud of sparks and flames. The spectacular fireworks display is supposed to scare away evil spirits for the start of the Chinese New Year.

ROOFTOP HOTEL

A one-room hotel opened in Paris, France, in 2007—perched on the roof of a museum. Designed as an art installation by Sabina Lang and Daniel Baumann, the Hotel Everland has stunning views of the Eiffel Tower, a king-size bed, a mini-bar, and breakfast delivered to the door. The creators say guests, who are allowed to stay for one night only, will be part of the exhibit.

GARDEN HIGHWAY
A Polish woman returned from holiday in 2007 to discover that the local council had built a road and a traffic island in her back garden. Alicia Ziemowit complained to Lodz Council, but was told that a change in the law meant officials could use private land for road-building without consent and without paying compensation.

VANISHING LAKE
In May 2007, a 5-acre (2-ha), 100-ft-deep (30-m) lake in Magallanes, Chile, disappeared in less than two weeks.

ELEPHANT ROCK
Located in the Valley of Fire in the Nevada Desert is a huge rock that is called Elephant Rock because it is shaped like an elephant. It was formed around 150 million years ago.

SUNNY OUTLOOK
An Italian Alpine village that never saw any sun in the winter months fixed the problem by installing a giant mirror. Lying at the bottom of a steep valley and surrounded by mountains, Viganella receives no direct sunlight between November and February, but in December 2006 the mirror—a sheet of steel measuring 26 x 16 ft (8 x 5 m)—was erected on a nearby peak to reflect sunlight onto the village square below.

PIGGY BANK
The Canadian town of Coleman, Alberta, boasts the biggest piggy bank in the world. The giant cash-collector has been converted from Ten Ton Toots, an old locomotive that used to pull cars in the town's coal mines.

CAVE DWELLERS
Centuries-old caves in Andalucia, Spain, have been connected to electricity and water supplies and fitted with modern furnishings in order to provide comfortable homes for people today.

BIG STAMP
An aluminum postage stamp measuring 8 x 6 ft (2.4 x 1.8 m) stands in Humboldt, Saskatchewan, Canada. It was built in 1999 in honor of former Canadian Prime Minister John G. Diefenbaker who, as a lawyer, defended many court cases in the town.

TREE BAR
A pub in South Africa is located in the hollow interior of a 6,000-year-old baobab tree. Inside, the tree is so spacious that the bar can hold 50 people and, because the 72-ft-tall (22-m) tree is still growing, so is the pub.

BEAR CODE
Smokey the Bear, the U.S. mascot for forest-fire prevention, has his own postal zip code for fan mail.

PRISON RODEO
The Louisiana State Penitentiary in Angola, which is home to 5,000 inmates, has thousands of acres of farm land, more than 1,500 cattle, a four-year theological seminary, its own radio station, a news magazine, and an annual rodeo.

KETCHUP CAPITAL
Already home to a 170-ft (52-m) ketchup bottle (in the form of a disguised water tower), Collinsville, Illinois, temporarily acquired a sister attraction in July 2007—a ketchup packet 8 x 4 ft (2.4 x 1.2 m), capable of holding around 127 gal (480 l) of ketchup.

SHRINKING SEA
The Aral Sea, located between Kazakhstan and Uzbekistan, has shrunk by 75 per cent during the last four decades as water is diverted for industry and agriculture.

LUXURY WASHROOM
A new public washroom in Chongqing, China, has more than 1,000 toilets, and covers an area of 3,350 sq yd (2,800 sq m). The four-story washroom has an Egyptian façade, gentle piped-in music, and even television. Some of the urinals are molded in unusual shapes—including a crocodile's open mouth!

CAVE VILLAGE
The village of Zhongdong in Guizhou, China, is located within a massive natural cave the size of an aircraft hangar.

NAKED LUNCH
In 2007, a restaurant in Greenville, Maine, offered a free prime rib sandwich to anyone willing to plunge naked into Moosehead Lake. The Black Frog Restaurant called its sandwich the Skinny Dip.

SLEEP CONCIERGE
The Benjamin Hotel in Manhattan is so concerned about its customers enjoying a good night's rest that it has its own sleep concierge. The hotel guarantees that guests will sleep as well as they do at home, or they get a free night's stay.

TREE HOMES

Canadian designer Tom Chudleigh has created a range of eco-friendly homes that can be suspended from trees or rock faces. Free Spirit Spheres are made from wood and coated in fiberglass to make them waterproof. Accessible only by rope bridge, the 11-ft-wide (3.6-m) houses can sleep four people and are fitted with a kitchen that is complete with microwave, refrigerator, and sink.

Index

Page numbers in *italics* refer to illustrations

ACKNOWLEDGMENTS

COVER (t/r) Mike Stanford WSDOT, (b/r) Image Copyright 2007 – Tony Rath Photography www.trphoto.com; BACK COVER Jon Cook and Miles Hilton-Barber; 4 Richard Wilson Turning the Place Over 2007 Courtesy Richard Wilson and Liverpool Biennial; 6–7 Fredrik Fransson; 7 (b/l) NASA; 8 (l) AFP/Getty Images, (r) Yang Fan/ChinaFotoPress/Photocome/PA Photos; 9 (t) ChinaFotoPress/Zhang Yanlin/Photocome/PA Photos, (b) Bournemouth News & Pic Service/Rex Features; 10 (r) Image Copyright 2007 – Tony Rath Photography www.trphoto.com; 11 Javier Trueba/MSF/Science Photo Library; 12 Mike Stanford WSDOT; 13 (t) Reuters/Darrin Zammit Lupi, (b) Reuters/Finbarr O'Reilly; 14 Richard Wilson Turning the Place Over 2007 Courtesy Richard Wilson and Liverpool Biennial; 15 (b) Cheng Xuliang/ChinaFotoPress/ Getty Images, (b/r) Reuters/Reinhard Krause; 16–17 Jon Cook and Miles Hilton-Barber; 18 (b/l) Yann Arthus-Bertrand/Corbis; 19 (t/l, t/c, t/r) Yann Arthus-Bertrand/Corbis, (b) Rykoff Collection/Corbis; 20 (b) Borys Czonkow/Rex Features; 21 (t, t/l) Reuters/Ho New, (b) Peter Foerster/DPA/PA Photos; 24 Ryan Froerer; 25 Victoria Simpson/Rex Features; 26 (t) Reuters/Chaiwat Subprasom, (b) Reuters/Sukree Sukplang; 27 (t) Reuters/Mariana Bazo, (b) AFP/Getty Images; 28–29 Timothy O'Rouke/Rex Features; 30 Reuters/Sergei Karpukhin; 31 (t) Ron Wurzer/Getty Images, (b/l, b/r) Jerome Favre/AP/PA Photos; 32 Sipa Press/Rex Features; 33 Rex Features

Key: t = top, b = bottom, c = center, l = left, r = right, sp = single page, dp = double page

All other photos are from Ripley Entertainment Inc.
Every attempt has been made to acknowledge correctly and contact copyright holders and we apologize in advance for any unintentional errors or omissions, which will be corrected in future editions.